D0754022

HOT OR NOT
20th-Century Male Artists

by Jessica Campbell

KOYAMA PRESS

DEDICATED TO EM KETTNER
AND WITH DEEP GRATITUDE TO
ANNE KOYAMA, ED KANERVA,
SHANNON STRATTON AND
AARON RENIER.

BIRTHING THE DANCE STAR:
GENIUS IN TWENTIETH-CENTURY ART-MAKING

by Leslie Barnardiston FitzRoy, Chief Curator at the Museum of Modern
& Contemporary Western Art, Rotterdam

"You must have chaos within you to give birth to a dancing star."
–Friedrich Nietzsche

Here is the first and finest introduction to make comprehensible the movements,
styles, and accomplishments of the most significant artists from the early 1900s
through the end of the twentieth-century. The artists' works and statements
examined herein illustrate the exciting tales of revolt, passion, and conflict that
characterized the last century's major art movements, and, without the least sac-
rifice of scholarship and with strict adherence to fact, this historical text remains
as riveting as fiction, as spellbinding as fantasy.

Consider the book you hold in your hands an indispensable modern classic–a
veritable prerequisite guide to the period that initiated the art of our time. These
men, the most famed figures in western art, are discussed in a straightforward
and lively way by one of the world's leading art critics, Jessica Campbell. Campbell's abilities as a writer and mastery of this large subject have enabled her to
bring it brilliantly to life in a text that, while not extensive, is richly filled with
historical and visual descriptions, anecdotes, and aesthetic evaluation. This book
answers questions about the nature of fine art, its merits, and how it is made.
It presents the simultaneous development of various artists, their relationships,
their feuds, their common struggles...It invites readers to peer into the minds of
modern masters—revolutionaries who challenged and eclipsed their predeces-
sors, and inspired generations of artists to come. These innovative, visionary
makers forever changed the course of western art, and their contributions are
honoured in the pages that follow. Its vivid descriptions, together with an en-
thralling chronicle of the twentieth century, make this the single most valuable
record of this period in art.

For the general reader, the precocious student of art, and the gallery visitor alike,
this is the authoritative tome that has long been needed; in it, you will find

examples of the work of leading artists. A pleasure to read from first to last, this book recounts lucidly and interestingly a long history of such artistic activity and accomplishment. Its many images of artworks provide not only a visual amplification of the text but also a generous sampling of the most memorable representational and abstract marks of all time. This text draws from innumerable documents, many little known and many never before published. These documents, extensively researched, include contemporary criticisms and eyewitness reports about the artists and their surroundings. It will, of course, come as no surprise to the seasoned art reader that the artists included within these pages created extraordinary and unforgettable works, but this text additionally details why and in what ways these works are original, and why they have been prized and valued by collectors and museumgoers for over one hundred years.

This text accounts for the most prevalent themes in modern art. The time and place in which the artist lives, the materials at his disposal, and the sorts of people represented in his paintings and sculptures each help to determine what kind of art he makes out of what he sees and how he thinks. Although his interpretation of a subject is very much his own, every artist is also the child of his particular culture and civilization. This text notes changes in style, subject matter, and technique, and examines each in the context of the times that produced them, with biographical information and brief accounts of the movements and other artists with which the artists were associated. In certain periods, paintings and sculptures of people may attempt to show what a person looks like, while in our own time the artist is certainly more interested in his own reactions to his model. In other periods, the artist may give an ideal beauty to his pictures of individuals, and in yet others he may be interested in showing only stylized, impersonal types. But, primarily, we must judge each work on its own artistic qualities, aware that often the artist is more concerned with his own creation than with merely representing what he sees. By understanding why artists at different times show their subjects in different ways, we learn a great deal about art, about the past, about our world, and, above all, about ourselves.

There are few characteristics that distinguish man from beast. Among these few, art production, the capacity to flatten and abstract the world such that it is appreciable by other men ranks near highest. Art has remained paramount in all cultures throughout all of human time. Such was certainly the case in the twentieth century, a century during which enormous technological advances propelled art forward to the degree that what we now appreciate as, if not beautiful, at least valuable, would be unrecognizable to our forefathers. These great men of the twentieth century–geniuses–flattened what had never yet been flat, angled what had previously been smoothed, and used media that had never before been considered art-worthy. But who were they?

What follows is the essential introduction to the art of the twentieth century and the preeminent artists it elevated to glory. Read on and be forever changed.

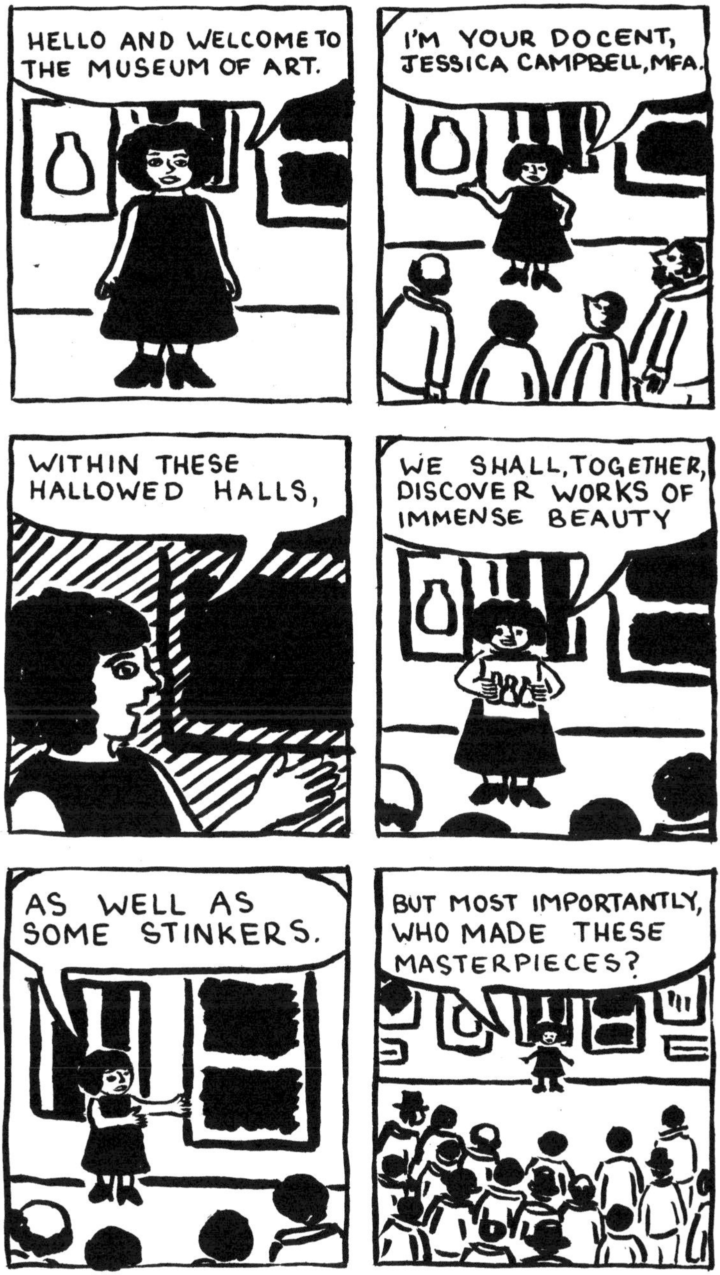
HELLO AND WELCOME TO THE MUSEUM OF ART.
I'M YOUR DOCENT, JESSICA CAMPBELL, MFA.
WITHIN THESE HALLOWED HALLS,
WE SHALL, TOGETHER, DISCOVER WORKS OF IMMENSE BEAUTY
AS WELL AS SOME STINKERS.
BUT MOST IMPORTANTLY, WHO MADE THESE MASTERPIECES?

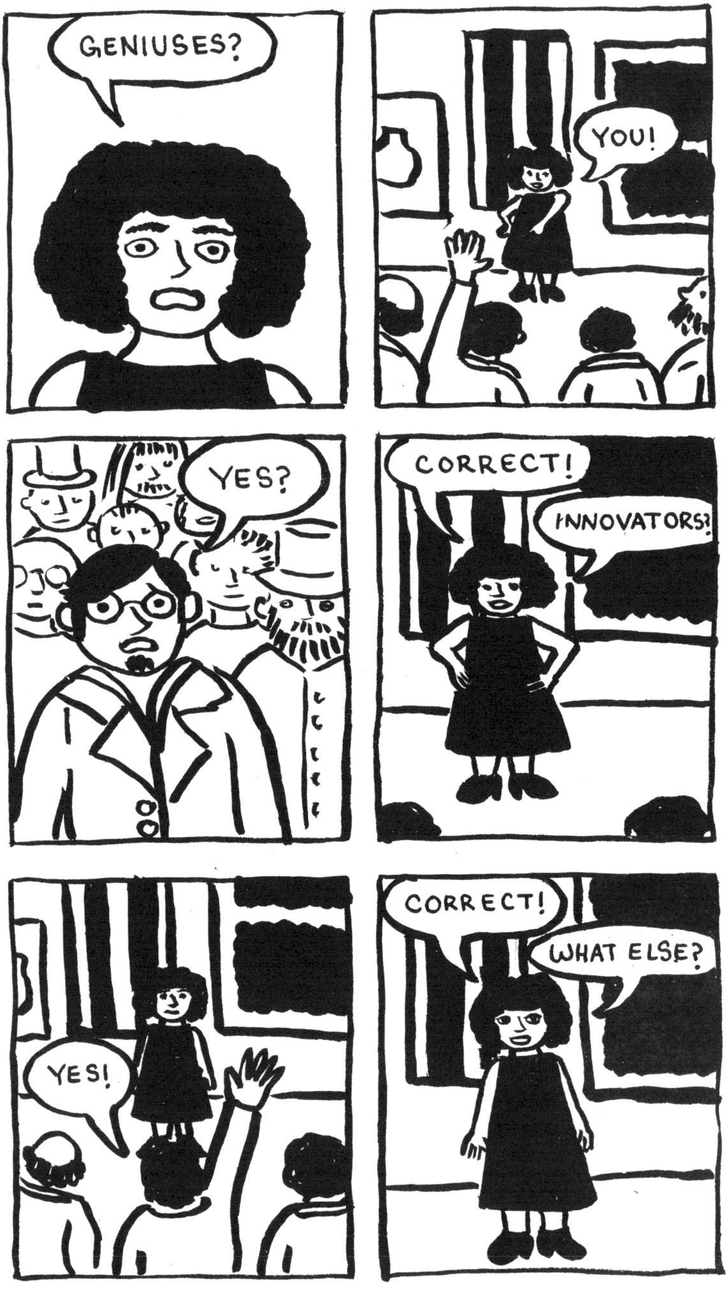
GENIUSES?
YOU!
YES?
CORRECT!
INNOVATORS?
YES!
CORRECT!
WHAT ELSE?

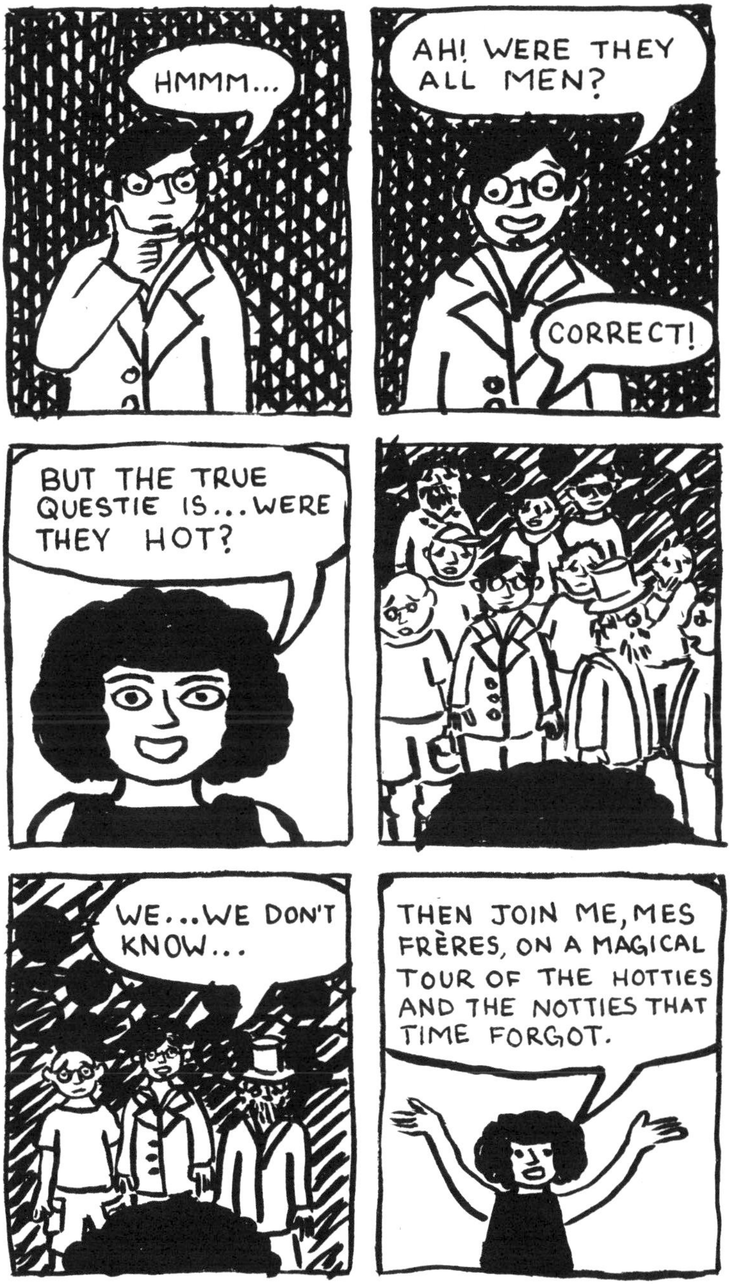
HMMM...
AH! WERE THEY ALL MEN?
CORRECT!
BUT THE TRUE QUESTIE IS...WERE THEY HOT?
WE...WE DON'T KNOW...
THEN JOIN ME, MES FRÈRES, ON A MAGICAL TOUR OF THE HOTTIES AND THE NOTTIES THAT TIME FORGOT.

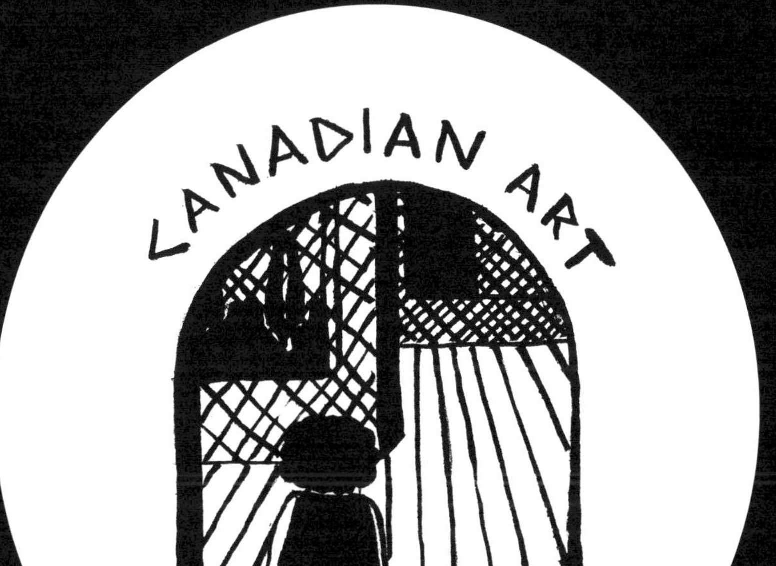
CANADIAN ART

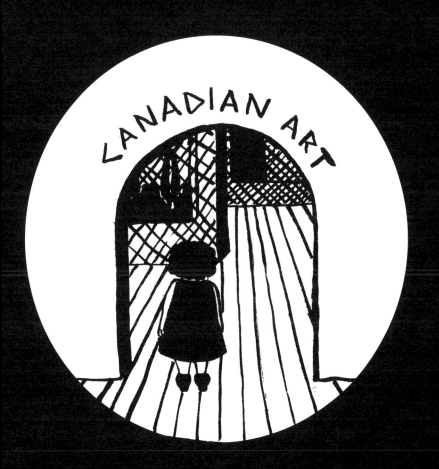

LAWREN HARRIS

AH YES, A REIMAGINING OF CANADA AS A SERIES OF JAGGED PENISES PIERCING AN ISOLATED LANDSCAPE. COULD BE A HOTTIE?

NOT

FINALLY I'VE DISCOVERED ALBERT
EINSTEIN'S LONG-LOST LOVECHILD
WITH A SEA ANEMONE.

P.É. BORDUAS

PAUL-ÉMILE BORDUAS, OR P.É. AS
I LIKE TO CALL HIM, WAS A
LEADER OF THE AUTOMATISTES,
A SIGNIFICANT PAINTING GROUP FROM
QUEBEC. HE WAS THE KIND OF
HOTTIE WHO'D TOSS YOU UP AGAINST
A BEAR AND MAKE ROUGH SEX TO YOU.

NOT

EDGAR ALLEN POE COSPLAY
WAS BIG IN 20th-CENTURY
QUEBEC.

DAVID MILNE

SIGH. CANADA, THERE IS NO WAY THAT THE MAN WHO MADE THIS PAINTING WAS BONEABLE. GET YOUR ACT TOGETHER, GUYS!

NOT

GET YE TO AN ISOLATED CANADIAN
FARMHOUSE AND OUT OF OUR
SIGHT LINE PLEASE, SIR!

PHILIP GUSTON

ALL RIGHT, CANADA, IMMA CALL
IN A PINCH HITTER. THAT'S
RIGHT, A SEXY LITTLE CANADIAN-
BORN AMERICAN BY THE NAME
OF PHIL GUSTON. FILL ME UP WITH
A GUST OF SEX WIND, PHIL!

HOT

IT'S HARD TO BELIEVE THAT
THIS SUPERMODEL MADE THOSE
EFF-ED UP PAINTINGS, BUT
DUDE HAD SOME B-A-G-G-A-G-E.

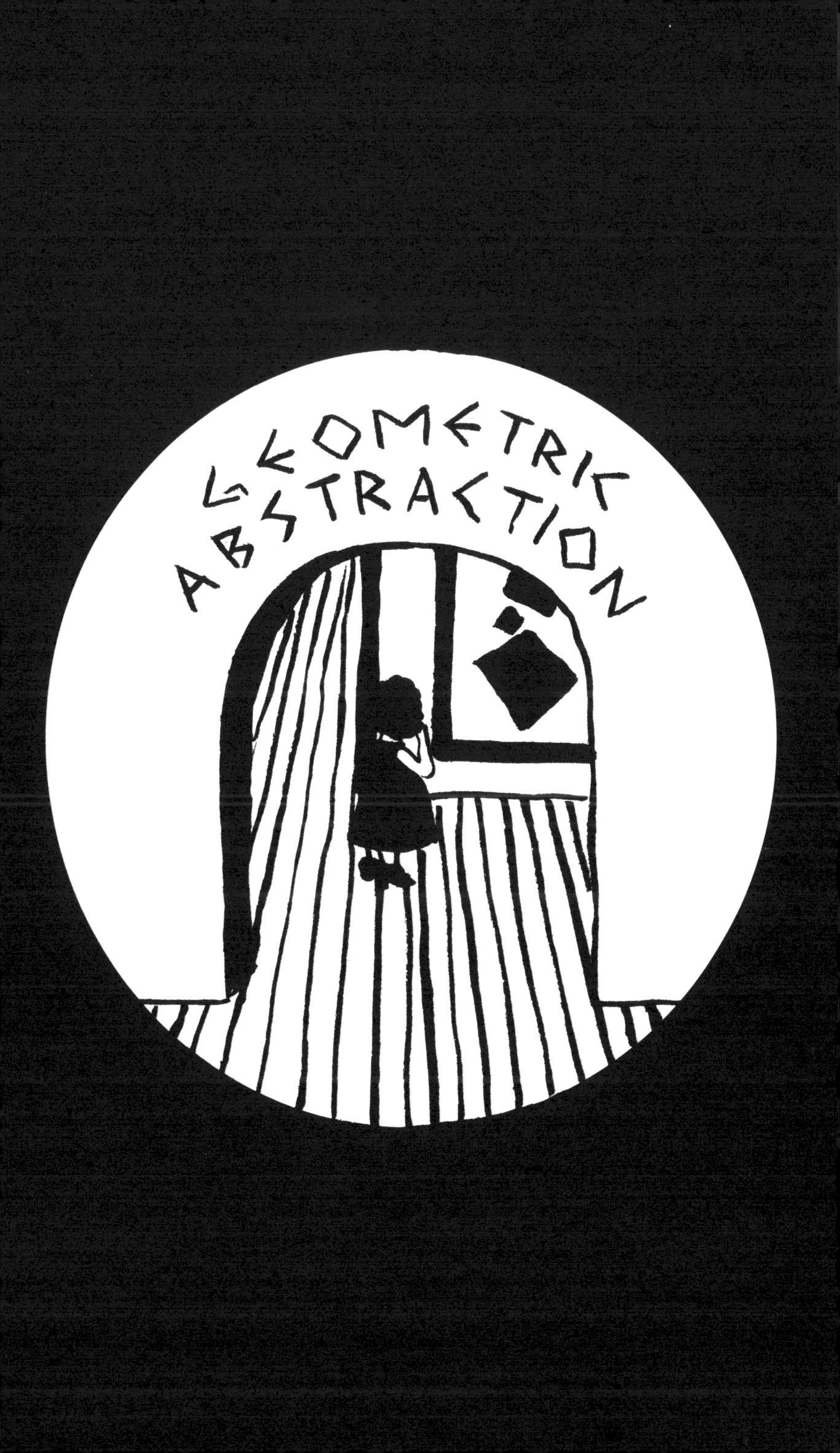
GEOMETRIK
ABSTRACTION

MALEVICH

THESE ARE THE PAINTINGS OF A
BROODING, COMPLICATED SEX MAN.

NOT

AND THIS IS THE FACE OF
AN ADULT BABY.

MONDRIAN

DUDE SPENT HIS LIFE
TRYING TO DISTILL THE WORLD
INTO SOME PERFECT SPIRITUAL
COMBINATION OF COLOURED SQUARES.
NOT HOT.

HOT

DANG! LOOKS LIKE THE PERFECT
COLOURED SQUARES WERE IN
THE MIRROR ALL ALONG.

BARNETT NEWMAN

HERE'S MY THOUGHT: BURLY, SHIRTLESS, CHOPPING TREES, SMOKING CIGS, MAKING PAINTINGS —THIS GUY WAS HOT.

NOT

UNLESS YOUR TYPE IS "SNOBBY SUPER MARIO."

SOL LEWITT

DUDE'S GOTTA BE A NOTTIE.
HE SEEMS LIKE A WEARER OF
MONOCLES AND ASCOTS WHO'D
SCOFF AT ANYONE WHO
DIDN'T APPRECIATE SQUARES
WITH ENOUGH GRAVITAS.

NOT

DID YOU KNOW THAT IN ORDER TO GET A TEMPORARY, MINIMUM WAGE JOB SCRIBBLING ON THE WALL PER LEWITT'S INSTRUCTIONS YOU NEED AN 80 K USD MASTER'S DEGREE?

ALEX CALDER

THESE SCULPTURES ARE FUN & FLIRTY,
BUT WAS THE SCULPTOR?

HOT

YESSSS! HE LOOKS LIKE A YOUNG DONALD SUTHERLAND, SON-IN-LAW OF THE CANADIAN HEALTH CARE SYSTEM. AND, WHAT ABOUT THAT CENTRE PART!

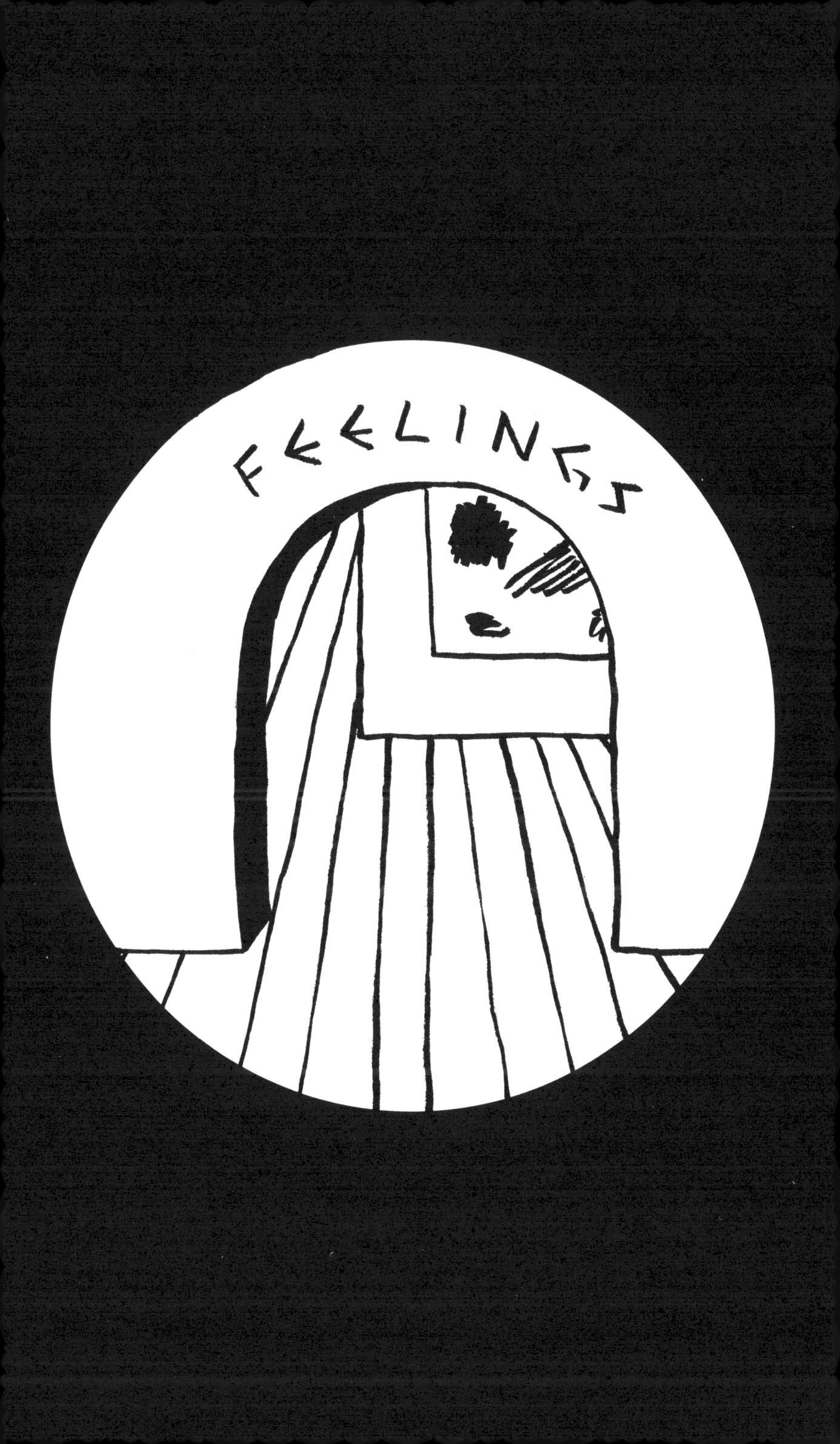
FEELINGS

MARK ROTHKO

ROTHKO'S ALL "WE COULD MAKE OUT, OR YOU COULD STARE AT THIS ORANGE BLOCK UNTIL YOU START CRYING."

NOT

I'LL TAKE THE ORANGE BLOCK, THANKS!

MORRIS LOUIS

THESE PAINTINGS FEEL
DELICATE AND SENSITIVE,
LIKE A FLOWER OR A
MAN WHO CRIES IN THE BATH.

UNCLEAR

WHILE I MAY KICK HIM OUT OF
BED FOR PAINTING IN THERE,
HE PROBABLY WOULD BE IN
THE BED TO START WITH.

CY TWOMBLY

MY GUESS? NO. SURE, I LOVE
THESE PAINTINGS, BUT I'M GOING
TO PRESUME THAT A FAT
GUY IN A BOWTIE MADE THEM.

HOT

BOOM! I STAND CORRECTED.

MATISSE

MY SUSPICION IS THAT SOMEONE
THINKING SO MUCH ABOUT COLOUR
AND FORM ON THE CANVAS
WASN'T THINKING SO MUCH ABOUT
HIS FORM AT THE GYM...

NOT

THIS IS PROBABLY WHY PICASSO
USED HIM AS A WINGMAN.

MORANDI

PRETTY SURE THAT WHEN MORANDI WASN'T PAINTING THESE VASES, HE WAS FILLING THEM WITH HIS OWN TEARS.

NOT

CONFIRMED!

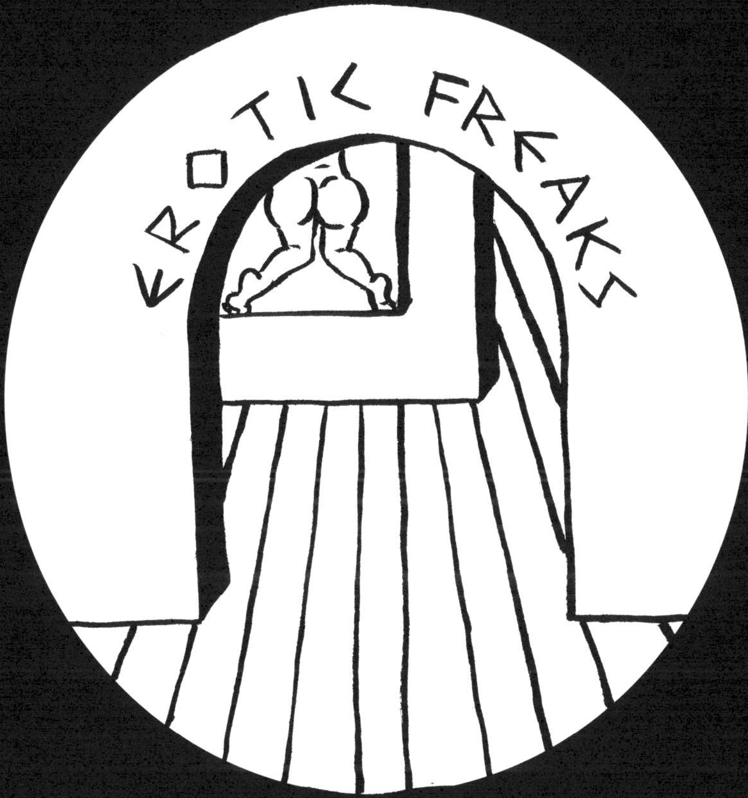
EROTIC FREAKS

HENRY MOORE

THIS MAN WAS PROBABLY
A CUBE. IS A CUBE HOT? IT
HAS A LOT OF ANGLES, AT
LEAST, WHICH SEEMS LIKE A
STEP IN THE RIGHT DIRECTION...

HOT

THIS EXPLAINS WHY MOORE NEVER SEEMED TO HAVE TIME ENOUGH TO TAKE AN ANATOMY CLASS: HE WAS FENDING OFF PRIVATE ANATOMY TUTORIALS FROM EVERY HUMAN WHO SAW HIM.

BALTHUS

OK, SO DUDE'S CLEARLY A PERV,
BUT DOES A PERV AN UGGO
MAKE? I SUSPECT IT MAY NOT.

HOT

MON DIEU! THIS FACE MAKES
ME WISH I WAS A CHILD
AGAIN! ALSO, A TIME TRAVELER.
SO I COULD BONE BALTHUS,
I MEAN.

MODIGLIANI

MODIGLIANI HAS BEEN IN EVERY
COLLEGE CO-ED'S BEDROOM SINCE
THE DAWN OF POSTERS, BUT ONLY
"AS A FRIEND," AND NO ONE ENDS
UP IN CONSISTENT FRIEND ZONE
PURGATORY BY BEING HANDSOME!

HOT

NEVER MIND! PAINT ME LIKE ONE OF YOUR MANGLED ITALIAN GIRLS, AMEDEO.

GUSTAV KLIMT

WHEN HE WASN'T PAINTING
(OR EVEN WHEN HE WAS) KLIMT
WAS IN THE PASSIONATE THROES
OF ORGY. SURELY A HOTTIE!

NOT

ON SECOND THOUGHT, THE
CAT/KAFTAN/CRAZY HAIR
COMBO COULD HAVE BEEN
ANTICIPATED.

PAUL GAUGUIN

"DEAR MOM—TAHITI'S GREAT!
IT'S WARM, THE LIGHT IS GOOD,
AND BEST OF ALL, THERE ARE LOTS
OF CHILDREN HERE FOR ME TO
HAVE SEX WITH."
—P. GAUGUIN, UNATTRACTIVE MAN

NOT

"DEAR MOM—YOU STILL THINK I'M HOT, RIGHT?"
— P. GAUGUIN, CHILD MOLESTER

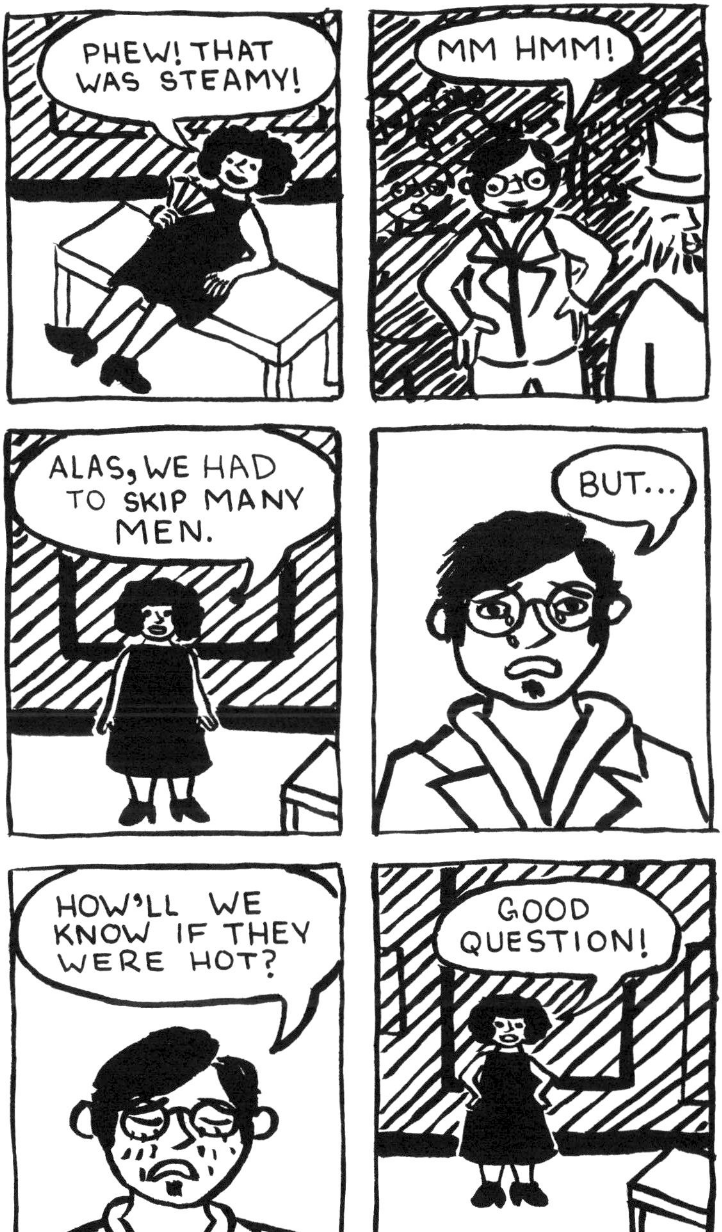
PHEW! THAT WAS STEAMY!
MM HMM!
ALAS, WE HAD TO SKIP MANY MEN.
BUT...
HOW'LL WE KNOW IF THEY WERE HOT?
GOOD QUESTION!

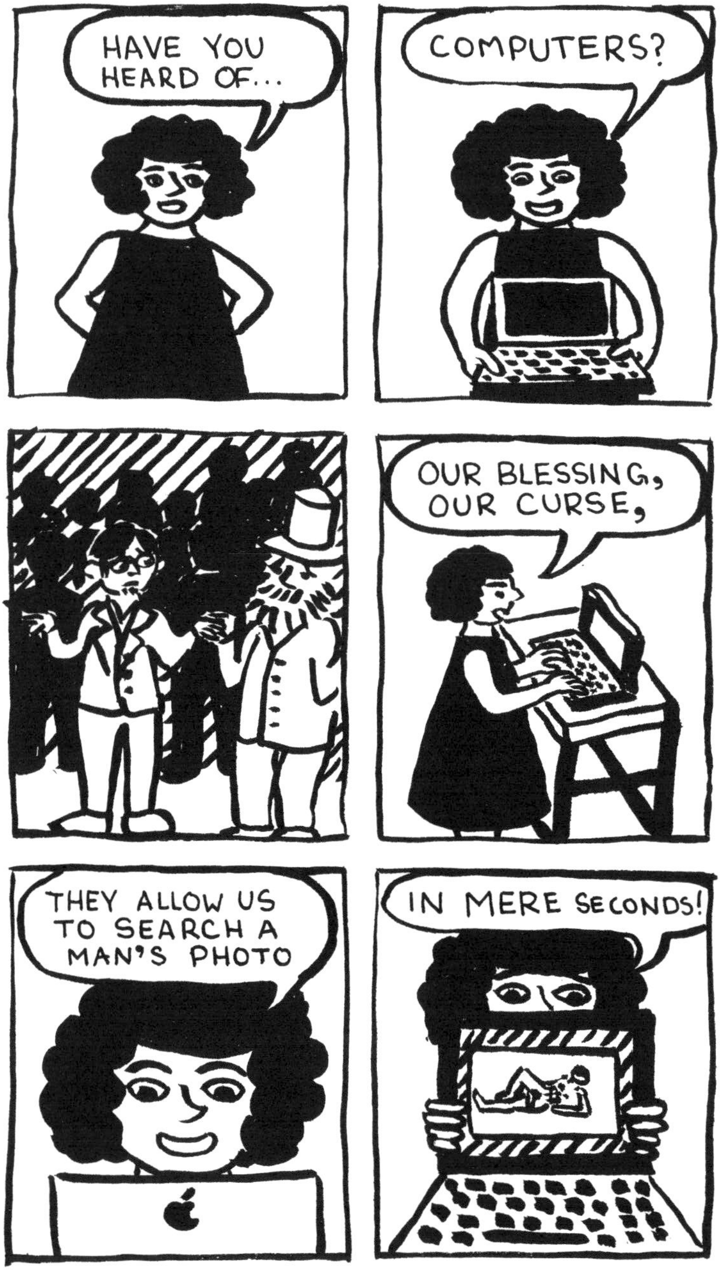
HAVE YOU HEARD OF...
COMPUTERS?
OUR BLESSING, OUR CURSE,
THEY ALLOW US TO SEARCH A MAN'S PHOTO
IN MERE SECONDS!

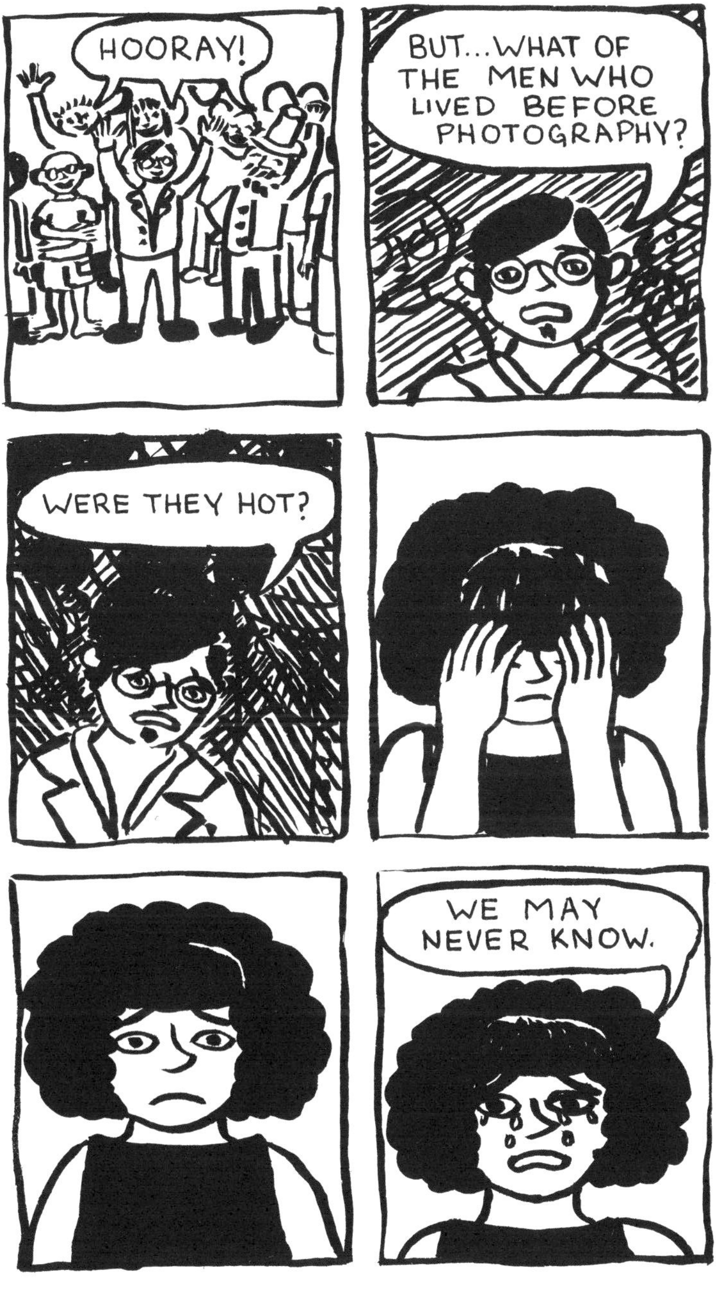
HOORAY!
BUT...WHAT OF THE MEN WHO LIVED BEFORE PHOTOGRAPHY?
WERE THEY HOT?
WE MAY NEVER KNOW.

All work is © 2016 Jessica Campbell | jessicacampbellpainting.tumblr.com
All rights reserved. No part of this publication (except small portions for review pur-
poses) may be reproduced or transmitted in any form without the prior written per-
mission of the publisher or artist. | Published by Koyama Press | koyamapress.com
First edition: September 2016 | ISBN: 978-1-927668-33-7 | Printed in Canada
Koyama Press gratefully acknowledges the Canada Council for the Arts and the
Ontario Arts Council for their support of our publishing program.